My Family

By

Grace Jones

Crabtree Publishing Company
www.crabtreebooks.com
1-800-387-7650

Published in Canada
Crabtree Publishing
616 Welland Avenue
St. Catharines, ON
L2M 5V6

Published in the United States
Crabtree Publishing
PMB 59051
350 Fifth Ave, 59th Floor
New York, NY 10118

Published by Crabtree Publishing Company in 2017

First Published by Book Life in 2016
Copyright © 2017 Book Life

Author
Grace Jones

Editors
Grace Jones
Janine Deschenes

Design
Danielle Jones

Proofreader
Crystal Sikkens

**Production coordinator and
prepress technician (interior)**
Margaret Amy Salter

Prepress technician (covers)
Ken Wright

Print coordinator
Katherine Berti

Photographs

All images from Shutterstock

Printed in Hong Kong/012017/BK20161024

Library and Archives Canada Cataloguing in Publication

OJones, Grace, 1990-, author
        My family / Grace Jones.

(Our values)
Issued in print and electronic formats.
ISBN 978-0-7787-3245-7 (hardback).--
ISBN 978-0-7787-3288-4 (paperback).--
ISBN 978-1-4271-1888-2 (html)

        1. Families--Juvenile literature. I. Title.

HQ744.J66 2016   j306.85   C2016-906649-5
                                     C2016-906864-1

Library of Congress Cataloging-in-Publication Data

CIP available at Library of Congress

Contents

Words that look like **this** can be found in the glossary on page 24.

What is a Family?

A family is a group of people who love and care for one another.

family members

People in a family are called family members. They are often **related** to each other.

No matter what size a family is, it is still a family.

Some families can be small. Other families can be big.

All families are different.

Parents

Parents are **adults** who look after you.

adults

children

Moms and dads are parents.

Some children have one parent.

You can have one mom or one dad.

Some families have two moms or two dads.

Brothers and Sisters

Some families have no children, one child, or many children.

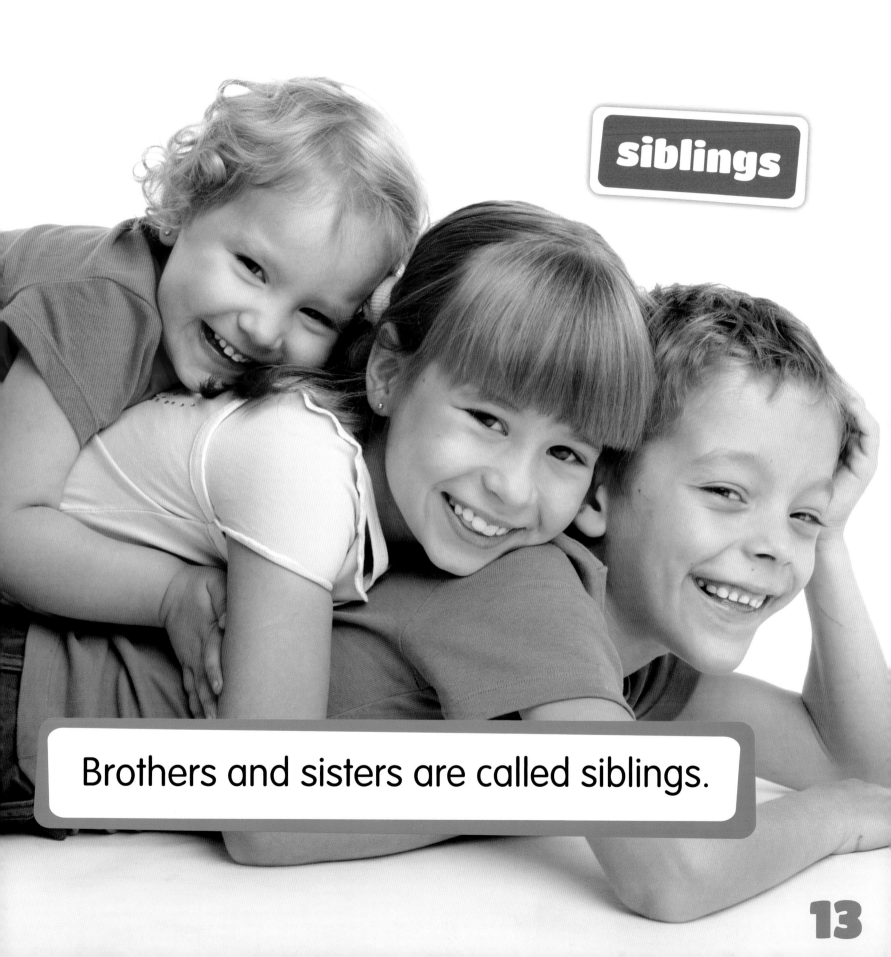

siblings

Brothers and sisters are called siblings.

This boy is older than his sister.

You can have younger and older siblings.

Two siblings born at the same time are called **twins**. Some twins look the same.

twins

15

Grandparents

grandparents

Grandparents are the parents of moms and dads. A grandfather is the father of a mom or dad. A grandmother is the mother of a mom or dad.

This grandfather is reading a story to his granddaughters.

Grandparents may help take care of their grandchildren.

Aunts and Uncles

aunt

uncle

Aunts and uncles are the siblings of mothers and fathers. An aunt is a sister of a mom or dad. An uncle is a brother of a mom or dad.

Sometimes your aunts and uncles might look after you.

19

Cousins

Your cousins are the children of your aunts and uncles.

Some families have many cousins.
Others do not include any cousins.

cousins

Role Models

A coach can be a role model.

Role models are people who you look up to and respect.

A parent can be a role model.

Role models can teach you the right ways to behave or how to do things.

Glossary

adults	People who are fully grown and not children
related	Coming from the same family members
respect	A feeling that someone or something is good and important
twins	Two siblings born at the same time to the same parents

Index